JOHN IZZO PhD

5 SECRETS

YOU MUST DISCOVER BEFORE YOU DIE

THE KEY TO LIVING A HAPPY AND MEANINGFUL LIFE

simple ▶ truths
small books. BIG IMPACT.

Photo Credits
Internals: pages 3, 5, 6, 7, 14, Monash/Shutterstock; page 12, Mykola Mazuryk/Shutterstock; page 19, Ollyy/Shutterstock; page 27, Johnny Adolphson/Shutterstock; page 29, Ricardo Reitmeyer/Shutterstock; page 32, Monash/Shutterstock; page 34, Gajus/Shutterstock; pages 40–41, Masson/Shutterstock; page 42, bikeriderlondon/Shutterstock; page 44, MitarArt/Shutterstock; page 46, Vasilyev Alexandr/Shutterstock; page 53, Sean Nel/Shutterstock; page 61, Joseph Ruscigno/Getty Images; page 65, Matthew Nigel/Shutterstock; page 67, Dasha Petrenko/Getty Images; page 68, LuckyBusiness/iStock; page 70, Strawberry Mood/Shutterstock; page 73, Nata Sdobnikova/Shutterstock; page 85, RubberBall Productions/Getty Images; page 88, Shulevskyy Volodymyr/Shutterstock; page 94, iStock/Getty Images; page 96, BlueSkyImages/Shutterstock; pages 98–99, Mirelle/Shutterstock; page 100, Frolova Elena/Shutterstock; page 109, Rock and Wasp/Shutterstock; page 119, nature photos/Shutterstock; page 120, Steve Cole/Getty Images; pages 122–123, Steve Cole/Getty Images; page 124, robbreece/Getty Images; page 126, Kamira/Shutterstock; page 129, Abel Mitja Varela/Getty Images; page 133, Nolte Lourens/Shutterstock; page 137, Blend Images–JGI/Jamie Grill/Getty Images; page 139, Sean Gladwell/Getty Images; page 145, Steve Krull/iStock; page 150, Chris Schmidt/Getty Images; pages 154–155, Spotmatik Ltd.

Published by Simple Truths, an imprint of Sourcebooks, Inc.
P.O. Box 4410, Naperville, Illinois 60567-4410
(630) 961-3900
Fax: (630) 961-2168
www.sourcebooks.com

Originally published in 2008 in the United States by Berrett-Koehler Publishers.

Printed and bound in China.
QL 10 9 8 7 6 5 4 3 2 1

Dedicated to my grandfather,

Henry Turpel, whose ring I wear

and whose legacy I carry on.

Contents

PROLOGUE

From the time I was a very young boy, I wanted to know the secrets to living well and dying happy. More than anything, I hoped that I would figure out what mattered before I died. When I was eight, this search was given a greater sense of urgency when my father died; he was only thirty-six. Life can be short, and we never know how much time we have to discover the secrets to happiness.

Early in my life, I had the privilege of spending time with people who were dying and discovered that individuals die very differently. Some people end their lives with deep satisfaction and few regrets. Others die with bitterness or with sad resignation at the life they might have lived. As a young person in my twenties, I set out to discover what separated these groups of people.

Many years ago now, a middle-aged woman named Margaret told me that she had tried to live her entire life from the perspective of an "old woman sitting on her rocking chair on the porch." Whenever she had a decision to make, she would imagine sitting on her porch as an old woman, looking back on her life. She would ask that old woman to advise her on the path she should take. It was a beautiful image.

In my mind, an idea began to germinate: Could it be that toward the end of life, we discover things about it that would have benefited us greatly if we had discovered them sooner? Would we learn some important things about living with purpose and finding deep happiness if we talked to those who had lived most of their lives already and had found happiness and meaning?

I believed that if I could identify people who had found the meaning in life and listened to their stories, the secrets to living well would emerge. I sought to identify several hundred people who had lived a long life and who had found happiness and wisdom with the goal of interviewing them to discover what they had learned about life.

I began by asking fifteen thousand people across the United States and Canada to send me their recommendations. I asked them: Who are the wise elders in your life? Whom do you know who has lived a long life and has something important to teach us about living? The response was overwhelming. Almost one thousand names were suggested. Through preinterviews, we identified 235 individuals representing a diverse group of people others had identified as wise. My hope was to learn the story of these people's lives and to learn the secrets of life—the secrets we must discover before we die.

The people we interviewed ranged in age from fifty-nine to 105. They were almost all from North America but were a diverse group in terms of ethnicity, culture, religion, geography, and professional status. Although many of the people we interviewed have achieved great success in their lives, our intent wasn't to seek famous people, but rather extraordinary people from all walks of life. We conducted one-to three-hour interviews with each of these people. Three of us conducted the interviews: Olivia McIvor, Leslie Knight, and myself. We asked questions such as: What brought you the greatest happiness? What are your regrets? What mattered, and what turned out not to matter? What were the major crossroads that made a difference in how your life turned out? What do you wish you had learned sooner?

This is a book for people at every stage of life. It is a book for young people who are just starting out on the journey of life. This is also a book for those in midlife, like me, who want to ensure that we discover what matters before it is too late, or for those in their later years who wish to reflect on their life experiences and discover ways to pass wisdom on to those who follow.

We do not have to wait until we are old to become wise. We can discover life's secrets at any age, and the sooner we discover them, the more fulfilling our life will be.

My conversations with these extraordinary people changed my life, and I hope they will change yours.

CHAPTER ONE

THE FIRST SECRET:
BE TRUE TO YOURSELF

"The greatest tragedy in life is to spend your whole life fishing only to discover that it was not fish you were after."

—Henry David Thoreau

CHOOSE TO LIVE LIFE AWAKE

 The first secret is to *be true to yourself* and *live with intention*.

IF WE ARE to follow our hearts and be true to ourselves, we must first make the choice to live our lives awake. Socrates said that the unexamined life is not worth living. There is another way to phrase that: unless you are *continually examining your life* to make sure it is on target, there is a very good chance that you will wind up living someone else's life, which means coming to the end of your life and realizing that you had followed a path that was not your own.

One woman, a seventy-two-year-old woman named Elsa, summed up the point of reflecting, of being awake. When I asked her to give me one sentence of advice for those younger than herself on finding happiness and purpose, she said, "I cannot do that. In order to tell a person the secret to happiness, I would have to sit down with them, find out who they are, what their dreams are. I say this because the secret to happiness is to be true to yourself." Each of us has a path that is most true to us, and *if we follow that path*, we find happiness. *The question that happy people ask is not whether they are focusing on what matters, but whether they are focusing on what matters to **them!***

THREE QUESTIONS THAT REALLY MATTER

BUT HOW DO we live true to ourselves? The secret is to *live with intention,* to consistently and regularly ask three critical life questions:

† Am I following my heart and being true to myself?
† Is my life focused on the things that really matter to me?
† Am I being the person I want to be in the world?

George was in his seventies and a retired professor of physics. For almost forty years, he taught young people over several generations, so it was natural for me to ask him what he noticed about life from teaching thousands of students. He said, "There was a chasm of difference between those students who were following their hearts and those who were not." Some students were following someone else's dream, maybe a parent's, or had simply wandered into a field that was not a good fit for the contours of their truest selves. These students always struggled. But others were following their hearts, and even if they were not the brightest students, they somehow worked through the challenges.

Often the seeds of not being true to our selves begin very early in our lives, when instead of asking what *we want to do* with our lives, *we compare ourselves* to others. One of the people I interviewed, Antony, was an eighty-five-year-old actor who was still directing and performing on a regular basis. Antony told me, "All I have done has been to be true to myself."

He told me that when he was very young, he observed the boys ahead of him in the grades above. Each year, he would pick one of them and think, *I want to be like him*. Then, one day, he realized that he was not any of those boys. The path to happiness was not in deciding which one he wanted to be like, but in determining what was most true to him. *"Don't try to be anyone else,"* *he advised. "Just make sure you are being you."*

IS YOUR LIFE MISSING THE MARK?

THE GREATEST SIN is to miss the mark of what you intended your life to be.

There are two levels to being true to one's self. First, on a day-to-day basis, am I living true to my soul? I like to tell people the problem with life is that it is so daily! A happy, purposeful life is the accumulation of many happy days. What became obvious to me as I was listening to the stories of people's lives is that wise people know what a good day is (a good day for them, that is). My grandfather, who was one of the wise elders in my life, used to talk about having a "good tired" at the end of a given day. He contrasted this with a "bad tired." He told me that a "good tired" was when you lived your life focusing on the things that really mattered to you. A "bad tired," he said, often comes even when it looks like we are winning, but we realize that we are not being true to ourselves. It seems to me that the first element of knowing ourselves is figuring out what makes up a "good tired" day for us.

Of course, following your heart and being true to yourself also involve larger questions. *Do my career and my work in the world represent my true self? Is my whole life truly my "path"? Am I being the kind of person I want to be in the world?*

FINDING YOUR DESTINY

"FOLLOWING YOUR HEART" means many things: it means doing work that suits your deepest interests, being true to yourself in the kind of life you choose (and being honest about what you want), and taking time to hear the small inner voice that tells you if you are missing the mark of your deepest desires.

Tom was in his sixties when I interviewed him. He is a Métis native, a tribe descended from native people in Canada who married French traders. When he was thirteen, he had an experience that changed his life.

Tom and some of his friends loved to skate on a large lake on the reservation. In the early days of winter in his fourteenth year, he and some friends headed out for a day of skating. Before they left the village, some of the elders warned them that the lake was not fully frozen, but with the invincibility of youth, they ignored the warnings. "I remember on the way out, we passed over a large crack in the ice, a crack that appeared each year, so we did not think much of it," Tom said.

As the daylight started to fade, the teenagers headed back to the village. When they came to the crack in the ice, Tom's three friends crossed gingerly over the crack, but Tom held back. Yelling to his friends to watch, he skated with all his might and leaped over the crack, but as he landed, the ice broke underneath him. Suddenly, he was beneath the surface of the frigid water. He looked up and swam toward the hole through which he had fallen. Grasping at the ice, he yelled to his friends for help. One by one, they tried to come to his aid, but each time he tried to climb up on the ice, it broke apart around him, forcing him back into a frigid nightmare.

Weary and shivering, he watched as his friends began to run to the village to seek help. Grasping at the ice one last time, he saw the last of his three friends turn to leave. Tom sank beneath the cold waters. He could feel his life slipping away from him. Looking up, he saw only darkness, having lost sight of the hole in the ice.

"I realized I was going to die. For some reason, all I could think about in that moment were the trees that lined the lake. They were aspen trees, and my people called them 'trembling aspens' because they have tiny leaves that flutter in the wind so that the entire forest appears to be trembling. As I began to feel my life slip away, all I could think about were the 'trembling aspens' and how I would never get to see them again. About to give up, I felt the trees calling me and looked up one last time, only to find a perfectly round hole in the ice that had not been there the moment before. Reaching up, I grabbed the ice, and it held. I could see my last friend just within earshot, and I yelled for him to help. He came back, held out his coat, and dragged me to safety."

At the time, he was simply grateful to be alive. Soon after, he began to wonder about the experience. "I kept wondering why I thought about the trees as I was dying. Why did I not think about my family, my parents, or my grandparents? It was a mystery that haunted me for many years."

Almost twenty years later, he shared the story with a medicine woman, a healer. She told him that the trees had saved him because it was his *destiny* to lead the ceremonies. In his tribe, the aspen trees were a central part of certain sacred ceremonies. The medicine woman told him, "You were born to be a healer." Tom realized that he had felt the calling to be a spiritual leader all of his life but had resisted the inklings. In that moment, he saw his true path. When he became a leader of the ceremonies, he was given his spiritual name: White Standing Buffalo. For the last thirty years, White Standing Buffalo has found his deepest sense of purpose in leading the dances and being a spiritual guide. He continued to make his living doing other things, but leading the ceremonies, and being a guide to others, became the true source of his meaning.

Each one of us has a trembling aspen on the lake of our lives, something that is most true to us. When we heed the sound of these yearnings, we find happiness and purpose; when we ignore them, we feel a hole in our hearts, like the hole in that frozen lake, that cannot be filled. We grasp at happiness, and each time, it breaks apart in our hands like the thin ice of that frozen lake. For some people, that true path is revealed as it was for Tom in one experience, but for many of us, the process of discovering who we are is much more subtle and happens over time.

In the interviews I conducted, Bob, who was just shy of sixty, revealed an inner journey that illustrates what happens when you are true to yourself. His mother had been a bird watcher, and his father, a gardener. When he was a young boy, they gave him two choices for his free time. "They told me I could go outside and play in nature, or I could go upstairs and read books, so I did both." He spent his time

wandering out in nature and observing wildlife, especially birds. In his room, he read books on nature and birds. From a very young age, he felt most at home outdoors. The natural world fascinated him and gave him great joy. When he was about ten, he announced to his mother that he was going to become a biologist, though he admits now that he probably had little idea what a biologist was.

He followed his instincts. Though he has worked in government, in the nonprofit sector, and as a volunteer, the common thread has been the wilderness. He looks back now with great satisfaction at his lifelong work fighting to preserve wild places. *From the beginning, it was nature, and being in it, that was his trembling aspen.*

FOLLOWING OUR HEARTS may involve quieting other voices that may want us to follow their dream. Ron, who was in his seventies when we met, had grown up in a family in which medicine was the profession of choice. His uncle had been a respected physician in the community, and when Ron decided to go into medicine, family and friends applauded his decision. Just before he was about to enter medical school, he went as a patient to see a gifted chiropractor. During treatment, he became acquainted with a discipline that believed in the power of the body to heal itself.

"I felt an immediate attraction to this profession and knew that it fit the contours of my soul. I knew I would be following my heart to do this. But chiropractic medicine was a bit of a mystery to people at the time, so when I announced my intention, my friends let me have it. But I knew it was my path, so I had to crowd out those voices. All of my life, I have known what to do. I think it is that way for most people; they know but have to have the courage to act."

He also told me that there were two keys to following your heart—*having the discipline to listen* and *the courage to follow*.

Does following your heart mean overturning your entire life and going in a completely new direction? What I discovered is that, in some cases, we must make a radical shift in our lives to follow our hearts. Ron had to walk away from medical school to become a chiropractor. But more often than not, the people

NEVER STOP ASKING WHETHER YOU ARE FOLLOWING YOUR HEART

I interviewed made small shifts and slowly aligned with their true path.

Jackie, sixty-six, went into banking at an early age and was quite successful. When she was in her forties, she attended a team session, and the participants were asked to introduce themselves by saying why they had gone into banking. When Jackie's turn came, she said, "I have been a banker for twenty-five years, but I always wanted to be a teacher. Business was my father's passion." The words came out of nowhere and surprised her with their clarity. "It was a shock to me.

It was not that I did not enjoy working at the bank, but I always knew that something was missing."

For weeks she considered her options. She had a great career at the bank and a lifestyle built around that work. Instead of quitting, she began to volunteer as a tutor on weekends at a local center for children. After many months of volunteering, she found that her bank sponsored a local organization to help children with learning challenges. She researched the organization and told her manager she wanted to be involved in that part of the bank's work. Over time, she became the main person at the bank responsible for connecting with the organization, and, on the bank's time, she made three missions over the years to Africa as part of that work. "Because I realized how important teaching was to me, I was able to integrate it into my life while still working there."

FOLLOW YOUR HEART

The secret I learned from my interviews is to *never stop asking whether you are following your heart,* whether the life you are living is truly yours.

Ron, the man who chose to become a chiropractor, put it this way: "You have to follow your heart, because to deny that is to deny everything. Of course you will make mistakes, you will miss the mark, but if you keep current with yourself, you move closer and closer to who you came here to be."

One of the things we must do to be authentic is to have the discipline to really listen to our heart. The discipline to listen means setting time aside to ask important questions. What many of these people had in common was that they took time on a regular basis to reflect on their lives.

We get so busy that we hardly have time to hear the voices of our own souls. *Sometimes it is only when we are forced to be quiet that we begin to see things more clearly.*

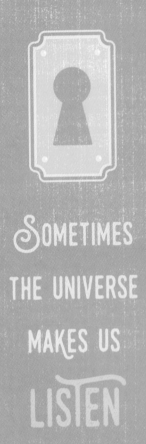

MY FRIEND DAVID was in his thirties when the universe caused him to stop and listen. He was a senior editor at a large business magazine, leading a very busy life—too busy for questions about whether he was living the life he truly wanted to live. Toward the end of his workday, he was sitting at his desk when he felt a pressure in his chest that soon became a mountain resting on him. In the emergency room, as he lay connected to monitors, he thought about his life. Quieted, with no distractions, he asked if he was truly following his heart. He thought about a simple question: If I live through this night, what must change?

He asked a nurse for a pencil and some paper, not knowing what the next twenty-four hours would hold. With Zen-like clarity, he wrote down five things:

† Play more
† Adopt a child
† Give back
† More time with family
† Start a foundation

"As I lay there that night, my life passed before my eyes. I did not think that my whole life had been wrong, but I knew there were some significant ways that I was not listening to my heart."

A few weeks later, David told me, "The good news is that I'm not dead; the bad news is that I am alive and have the list!" The universe had put him on his back to reflect and forced on him the discipline to listen. Now he would have to have the courage to act.

What about those five things he had written on that piece of paper? He knew he was working too hard and needed more time for enjoyment. His dream of adopting a child was too important to put off. He wanted to spend more time with his family. He did not even know where the words "start a foundation" came from.

For the next two years, he carried the list around with him. He adopted a son. He played a great deal more. He moved closer to family, and sure enough, two years later, he started a foundation in his father's name.

Of course, we do not have to wait for an illness to create a list we could make any day of our lives. If you were lying on that hospital bed right now, what would be on that short list? To be more true to myself, I must…

George, the physics professor, gave me one more piece of professorial advice: "I always told my students on the first day of class: Don't count on cramming. Don't count on coming to the end of the semester and trying to cram in months of work; it just won't happen. Life is like that. So many people keep saying someday they will follow their hearts, be the person they want to be in the world. If there is something you need to do, get to it. *If you follow your heart and stay current with yourself, it works **out**."*

That is the first secret: **be true to yourself**.

"*A human being may be the one creature on earth who can miss their calling. What matters most is to know what matters most to YOU. If you answer that question and live true to it, you will be happy and the world a better place.*"

—John Izzo

CHAPTER TWO

THE SECOND SECRET: LEAVE NO REGRETS

"The bitterest tears shed over graves are for words left unsaid and deeds left undone."

—Harriet Beecher Stowe

Regret is possibly the one thing we all fear the most, that we might look back on our lives and wish we had done things differently. In my experience, death is not what we fear the most. When we have lived life fully and have done what we hoped to do, we can accept death with grace. What we fear most is not having lived to the fullest extent possible, to come to the end of our life with our final words being "I wish I had."

If we want to find true happiness and purpose, we must embrace the second secret: *leave no regrets*. To leave no regrets, we must live with courage, moving toward what we want rather than away from what we fear. We must overcome the inevitable disappointments that life hands us.

We asked each of our interviewees to tell us about the major crossroads in their lives, times when they made a decision to go in one direction or another and how that decision made all the difference in terms of how their lives turned out. When they reflected on those crossroads, they almost always noted an element of risk involved—they had to move toward something they wanted, in spite of fear.

It became evident that, at the end of our lives, *we will not regret* risks we took that did not work out as we hoped. Not one person said they regretted having tried something and failed.

Yet, most people said they had not taken enough risks. Many of those I interviewed told me that what we call "mistakes" often turn out to be the moments of greatest learning.

We can never guarantee success in our lives, since every attempt holds within it the possibility of failure. If we love, there is always the risk of rejection. If we follow a dream, there is always the possibility of falling short. We cannot guarantee success, but *we can guarantee failure merely by choosing not to try at all*. Choosing to take a risk, however small, can have far-reaching implications in the course of a human life.

A LIFE OF NO REGRET MEANS RISKING MORE

DONALD WAS EIGHTY-FOUR years old when I interviewed him. A psychologist by training, he looked back on a rich, meaningful life. He had few regrets. One of the greatest sources of happiness in his life had been his fifty-six-year marriage to his wife, who had died six years before our interview. When I asked him about crossroads moments in his life, he immediately took me back sixty-two years to a college dance.

"I was a shy young man, especially when it came to talking to the ladies. In my freshman year at a college dance, I saw a beautiful young woman across the room. She was wearing a cream sweater, her hair was soft, and she had a wonderful smile. The moment I laid eyes on her, I knew she was the one. This was the woman I was going to marry."

As young Donald looked across that room, he knew she was a popular girl. He knew he risked ridicule and embarrassment if he went up to her and she rejected his offer to dance.

"Taking a big gulp, I walked right over and told her she was the woman I was going to marry. This came as news to her, and she wasn't terribly impressed but danced with me anyway. One dance turned into two and then three. Over the next few weeks, I had to pursue her quite a bit before she realized this dance would last a lifetime."

WE MUST ALWAYS

MOVE TOWARD

WHAT WE WANT

RATHER THAN

AWAY FROM

WHAT WE FEAR

Such a small decision—the decision to risk failure reaching for what he wanted—turned out to be one of the most important decisions of Don's entire life. The marriage defined his life in many ways, and even six years after her death, he told me, "There is not one day that I don't feel her presence around me."

Yet, I kept wondering what would have happened if the fear of embarrassment had won out that day, if he had sealed his failure by taking no action. At the age of eighty-four, would he look back and regret not having walked across the room and tried?

Of course, not every small act of courage winds up defining our lives or being a major crossroad in our search for happiness. But since we cannot know in advance the risks that matter, we must always move *toward what we want* rather than *away from what we fear*.

One of the most poignant moments in the interviews came when I was talking with a woman named May, who was in her seventies. She told me how she had been working on six different books for the last several decades. Yet none of them was complete.

When I asked her why she had all these unfinished books, she said, "All of my life, I have left things unfinished. I thought it was just procrastination. But as I reflect on it, I believe I have not finished these books because if I ever do finish them, I would have to let someone read them. Perhaps they will tell me that I cannot write. I suppose it is the fear of rejection that has kept me from finishing."

My heart went out to her. Seventy-one years old and, because of fear, she might never complete the books that have been inside her all her life. Of course, the rejection she fears could become reality, but it is hard to imagine anything worse than dying with your story trapped inside you.

But many of us do that very thing. *For fear of rejection, or failure, or because we are not sure we can succeed, we die with our book, our dreams, our story inside us.*

When I asked two hundred people what they would go back to tell their younger selves, one of the most common answers was to take more risks. *People often identified moments when they took a perceived risk as a significant step on the path to happiness.*

THE SECRET TO NO REGRETS

THIS LEAVES US with a more important question: How do we take more risks in the direction of what we want? How can we live so as not to regret the steps we did not take?

Perhaps my greatest teacher was a woman in her seventies who had grown up in Germany during World War II. As she looked back on her life, she told me that the most important crossroads were times when she had to act with courage. For example, after the war, things were very difficult in Germany. At the age of twenty-two, Elsa took the first of many significant risks in her life. She decided to move to Canada and start a new life. At the time, she did not know anyone in Canada, had no job prospects, and did not know the language. She told me that although the decision felt very risky at the time, it was *the* turning point in her life.

When I asked her how she took important risks, she told me, "Whenever I had a risk I was considering, I would begin by imagining the highest possible good that could occur by taking that risk. Then I would imagine the worst possible thing that could happen if I took the risk. I would ask if I could handle the worst thing, and every time, I knew I could. If I moved to Canada and it did not work out, I might wind up broke and alone. I knew I could always come home. But then I imagined the highest possibility, that I would start a new life, that I would make many friends, find love, and raise children in this new country. Then, I held that image in front of me. Whenever I began wavering, I would imagine the greatest good I was striving for. I would always remind myself that walking away from the good that was possible was far worse than the consequences of failure."

Many of us live our lives in quite the opposite way. When faced with a risk, we imagine the worst things that could happen and hold these thoughts in front of us.

When I was growing up in New York City at the height of the Cold War, the threat of nuclear war was very real. Every few months, we practiced air-raid drills, preparing for the arrival of "the bomb." To this day, I remember the fear I felt, that one day I would be sitting at my desk and life as I knew it would end. When the air-raid drill sounded, the teacher would have us all get under our desks.

One time, during a drill, a friend of mine named Kenny walked over to the window while the rest of us cowered under our desks. The teacher said, "What are you doing? Get under your desk!" Kenny responded, "Mrs. Brown, if they are going to get me anyway, I'd rather stand up and watch the bright light than hide under my desk!"

Many of us live our entire lives hiding under the desk, believing that failure and rejection are the worst that can happen to us. *Yet these interviews brought me to a different conclusion— the thing we ought to fear most is the regret of having not tried.*

CHOOSE THE PATH THAT MAKES THE BEST STORY

HOW DO WE keep from living a life with regret? I've mentioned Margaret, who tried to live her life from the perspective of an old woman. Whenever she had a decision to make, she asked herself this question: "When I am an old woman sitting in my rocking chair thinking about my life, what decision will I wish I had made?"

She told me that in almost every case, the path she should take became clear to her. Deena Metzger, well-known author and spiritual guide, put it this way: "Choose the path that makes for the best story."

This is an interesting but simple way to live a life with no regrets. We continually look ahead and ask ourselves: *When I come to the end of my life, will I regret the step I am about to make?*

As I listened to the stories of people's lives, I realized that some of my own most significant regrets have to do with the opportunities I turned away, often because of fear.

This past year, a good friend of mine offered me the opportunity to spend a month in East Africa with fifteen other midlife men, meeting with tribal elders and camping in the wilderness. This was a dream come true, but it was my busiest time of year, and I would have to turn down a significant amount of work to take the trip. This time, I paid a visit to that old man on the porch. He told me, "When you are my age, you won't miss the money you lost this month, but you will carry Africa in your heart."

I took the trip, explored several fascinating cultures, saw amazing wilderness, and missed the presence of my family, which reminded me of how much they mean to me. While in Tanzania, I sat with tribal elders and germinated the idea for this project. My worry about interference with a busy schedule almost got in the way of one of the most important experiences of my life.

The most important thing about this second secret is to make sure we try for the things we want in our lives, because we are unlikely to regret trying and failing. The second most important lesson is that if there is a relationship that must be healed, heal it now. *When I asked people about regrets, most of them spoke about people in their lives, about issues not resolved, words not spoken, broken relationships never healed.*

LIVING
AS IF YOUR
TIME
IS SHORT

OVER THE YEARS, I have led many personal and leadership development retreats with my dear friend Dr. David Kuhl, a gifted physician and author. During workshops, we conduct an exercise where we ask people to imagine they only have six months to live. We tell them they cannot be certain whether these will be healthy or difficult months.

"Pretend," we say, "that on that day six months from now, you will die. What are five things you must do before that time?" People most commonly write about relationships that must be healed.

Once people have finished their lists, we ask, "If you had only six months left to live and the things on your list are things you must do, are they not important enough to do regardless of how much time you have left?"

We are already in this position. We may indeed have only six months to live, and asking ourselves how we would live our lives if we had only that time left is a great path to living with no regrets.

Lucy, now in her seventies, had been estranged from her mother for many years. They hardly talked for the last twenty years of her mother's life. "I wish I would have reached out to her sooner and tried to show her how to love. I would say to anyone who will listen, if there is something you have to say, say it sooner, even if you don't feel ready."

Of course, there is no perfection in this life, and there will be some regrets, no matter how carefully we live our lives.

REGRETS
ARE BEST
LET GO

A COMMON TRAIT among those identified as having found happiness was their ability to dust themselves off and get back up. It is not that they had had fewer disappointments than others did, but they refused to allow setbacks to defeat them. *Perhaps what often determines our happiness in life is the step we take after a setback.* There will always be setbacks, and these setbacks often require us to risk again. To love after we have been hurt or lost. To try even after we have failed or been rejected.

It is often said that we cannot for-give others if we cannot first forgive ourselves. Though one of the secrets is to leave no regrets, most of us will have a few. So we must choose to heal the regrets we do have, to bathe them in forgiveness, to know that, in most cases, we did the best we knew how to do at the time we acted. It is a sign of our wisdom that we can embrace regret and let it go. Indeed, one difference I noted between the wise elders and the less happy people we interviewed was how they dealt with regret in

their lives. The happiest people had come to peace with their lives, whereas unhappy people dwelled on regret and missed opportunities.

What chances would you take if you knew you had only one year to live? Are you playing your life safe hiding under the desk, or are you standing by the window to watch the show? *If you look at your life from the perspective of an old person sitting on a porch, what will you wish you had done?*

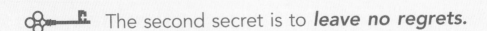

The second secret is to *leave no regrets.*

CHAPTER THREE

THE THIRD SECRET:
BECOME LOVE

"Love is life. And if you miss love, you miss life."

—Leo Buscaglia

David, now in his seventies, told me about an experience he had when his father was dying. The family had gathered from many parts of the world to share his father's final days. During those last few days, his father made no mention of cars, houses, or any other possessions he had acquired during his lifetime. Rather, he surrounded himself with photos of special times from his life—weddings, births, family trips, and times with friends. Watching his father die, David concluded, "At the end of our lives, when we only have a short time left, love is really the only thing we will care about." For many years, David carried this image with him, an image that guided how he has lived his life.

Our several hundred conversations clearly show that love, both the giving and receiving of it, is the fundamental building block of a happy, purposeful human life.

The most important thing I learned about the secrets to a happy and purposeful life was that it is not just the *receiving of love* that matters. The secret to happiness and purpose is also to *be a loving person*. So the third secret we must discover about life before we die is to *become love*.

LOVE
AS A
CHOICE

IT IS NECESSARY to make a distinction between the *emotion of love* and the *choice to love*. Love is commonly perceived in our society as only an emotion. We say things such as "she is passionately in love with him," that we "love golf and pizza," that we "love to party," and on it goes—but we are referring to the emotion of feeling love. Yet, as I listened to the interviewees, I began to realize that when they spoke of how important love was in their lives, they were defining love more as a choice than an emotion.

Although we may not have the ability to "feel" love at will, we have the power at every moment to choose to become love. We live out this secret in three ways. *First, we choose to love ourselves. Second, we choose to act with love for those closest to us (family and friends). And finally, we must choose to become love in all our interactions.*

FIRST, LOVE YOURSELF

THE FIRST WAY we live this secret is by choosing to love ourselves. Unless we fundamentally choose to see ourselves as worthy, we cannot find happiness. The love of self is fundamental to being a spiritually healthy human being. For some of us, self-love may come naturally because our upbringing and early experiences gave us a deep sense of our own self-worth, but for others, the love of self comes with difficulty.

They say that we are what we eat, but from a spiritual point of view, we are what we think. Human beings have an average of forty-five thousand to fifty-five thousand thoughts per day, a veritable nonstop inner conversation. Many of them have a large impact on how we see ourselves. For example, every time we tell ourselves "I am a loser," "I am not lovable," "I am unattractive," "I have to prove myself to others," "I am not a good parent," "I am not a good person," we are committing acts that undermine the love of self.

Lee, seventy-eight, spent a lifetime trying to understand the human brain and how we hypnotize ourselves with our own thoughts. He told me, "Often, when we are young, we get programmed, we get hypnotized, with a kind of toxic view of the self. Through our own thoughts, we also have the power to dehypnotize ourselves by choosing to plant flowers or to plant weeds. The subconscious treats every thought as a prayer."

When he said this, I realized that most of the people I was interviewing spent most of their time planting flowers. The love of self is about what we feed our minds. And we have power over this internal conversation.

There is a wonderful story in the Navajo tradition. An old Navajo told his grandson that sometimes he feels there is a fight going on inside him. "It is a fight between two wolves. One wolf is evil. It is the wolf of anger, envy, sorrow, regret, greed, arrogance, self-pity, guilt, resentment, inferiority, superiority, fear of healing my body and mind, fear of succeeding, fear of exploring what has been said by others to be truth, fear of walking in others' moccasins and seeing glimpses of their reality through their eyes and their hearts, using empty excuses that my heart knows to be false. The other wolf is good. It is the wolf of joy, peace, love, hope, serenity, humility, kindness, empathy, caring for those who have helped me even though their efforts have not always been perfect, the willingness to forgive myself and others, and realizing that my destiny is in my hands."

The grandson thought about it and asked, "But, Grandfather, which wolf wins?" His grandfather replied, "The wolf that I choose to feed."

The first part of this secret is to feed the right wolves within ourselves.

MAKE LOVE A PRIORITY

THE SECOND PART of this secret is to choose to act with love toward those closest to us and to make loving relationships a priority in our lives. When I asked people what the greatest happiness was for them, their first responses almost always referred to spouses, children, parents, and friends. Again and again, I saw that those people who focus on the development of deep personal relationships in their lives become happy. Conversely, when I asked people about regrets, the first responses were about relationships as well, either a lack of priority given to them or a feeling of having not acted with love toward those who matter most. Many years ago, a bitter older man told me, "I spent most of my life on things. People always came in a distant second in terms of my priorities. Now I realize that my BMW doesn't come to visit me in the nursing home."

One of my favorite interviewees was a sixty-two-year-old man named Ken. He had been a barber in the small community of Waukon, Iowa, for forty-two years.

Being a barber in a town of about four thousand residents is akin to being a priest or a minister, except that the profession of barber crosses all affiliations and boundaries. It was obvious from the moment I began talking with Ken that not only did he know a fair amount about living a fulfilling and purposeful life, but he also had been a good student in years of intimate observation.

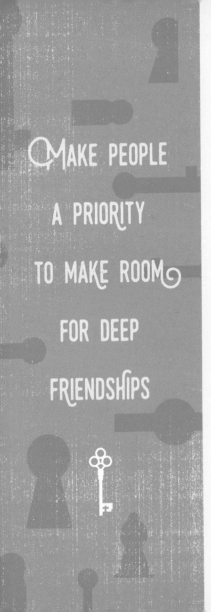

MAKE PEOPLE A PRIORITY TO MAKE ROOM FOR DEEP FRIENDSHIPS

"You watch long enough, and you figure out what makes people happy," he said. "I noticed that if you have love in your life and a job that gives you purpose, you will be a happy person." It didn't take long to figure out that Ken had both the love of family and friends and a job that gave him a deep sense of purpose, beyond the task of cutting hair. For him, the job provided the opportunity to serve others and to develop deep friendships.

He told me the best advice he had ever gotten was from his wife's father, who told him very early in their relationship that "there will be uphill battles and downhill ones; it is all part of life. Your checkbook is not your success—the people you meet and influence in your life will be your success."

Friends, family, and other people had always been the most important thing in his life.

The second part of this secret is to make people a priority, to make room for deep friendships, and to ask each day whether you are acting with love toward those who are close to you.

Of course, it sounds easy to make people a priority and to act with love toward them. What I discovered is that, although this particular secret is not really secret, many people still often put material things before people, and in our busyness, we forget to act with love toward those closest to us. Many of the deepest regrets people had were about not truly being there for the people they loved.

Dave, a sixty-five-year-old retired bank executive, told me a poignant story. When I asked him what the best piece of advice was that he had ever received about life, "When I was in my forties, my boss's wife died of cancer. When he came back to work after a few months, he stopped me in the hall one day, grabbing me by the arm. 'Dave,' he pleaded with me, 'spend more time with your wife; spend more time with your wife.' He had no reason to say that to me, really. But I believe it was the best piece of advice anyone ever gave me. And if he could see me now, he would probably tell me that I did not heed it."

He went on to tell me that he wished he could go back and place a higher priority on relationships. Although he deeply enjoyed his work, he felt he had sacrificed too much in order to be successful. Dave was typical of many of the people we interviewed. The importance of people in their lives was often lost in the busy pursuit of career and livelihood.

People often look back with regret about having allowed anger or unimportant things to get in the way of loving relationships.

Would I too look back and wish I had been more present and more loving? It occurred to me that becoming love to those who matter most to us is often about seeing the larger picture, the love that matters more than things.

A few years ago, when my children were in their early teens, my wife told me she was buying a used trampoline from our next-door neighbor. It was large and very old (and quite unattractive). We had just renovated our backyard, and the thought of having that ugly thing smack in the middle of it irked me. Once the trampoline was in place, I expressed my displeasure to my wife. She was unimpressed and told me that I ought to rethink my priorities. I looked out my bedroom window and let out an audible "argh" at the new view. I let everyone in the family know of my distaste.

Hours later, I heard the loud laughter of my children bouncing with glee on the new acquisition with their friends. It occurred to me that they would be gone soon, living their own adult lives. Surely I would miss those voices, the echo of hearty laughter, far more than I now missed the beauty of my yard. *It was an important lesson. In each moment, we must ask what really matters and act accordingly.*

CHOOSING
TO SEE
OTHERS WITH
KINDNESS

IN TALKING WITH the people I interviewed, I learned the importance of choosing to see those around us with kindness. Some time ago, I met an eighty-five-year-old marriage counselor named Maggie. For more than fifty years, she listened to husbands and wives talk about each other. When I asked her what she noticed in all those years of counseling couples, she told me, "When people are first together, they focus almost entirely on the things they like about the other person. But over time, people focus more and more on the things that irritate them about the other person rather than what they like. If people would just turn that ratio around, most marriages and families would be so much better."

Jim, eighty-six and still happily married after sixty-five years, had lived this simple secret. Though he had a great career in the military, when asked what mattered, he kept coming back to the subject of his wife.

Every year for their entire married life, he sends her red roses on the anniversary of their first date rather than their wedding anniversary. "It is as much for me as it is for her. When I send them every year, it reminds me that, through all the ups and downs of marriage, I must never forget why I fell in love with her in the first place." Perhaps each of us must continually look for the red roses in those we love, focusing on the things that are good about them.

A study by a major university showed that, in the average home, the ratio of negative to positive messages is fourteen to one. For every one positive comment we make to a person in the family, we make almost fourteen critical comments. A similar study showed that one of the common elements in long-term, happy marriages was a seven-to-one positive-to-negative ratio in communication.

It is in our power to change that ratio. At each moment, we can choose to become love and affirm one another. We can choose to see the larger picture.

When we choose to become love in all the encounters of our lives, when we choose love and kindness as our way in the world, happiness finds us. *When we give love away, it comes back to us in the form of happiness.*

Do
GOOD
IF YOU CAN,
BUT ALWAYS
DO NO HARM

BANSI, SIXTY-THREE, WAS an immigrant from Tanzania, now living in Canada. Raised as a Hindu, she felt that the choice to be kind was at the center of a happy life. When I asked her about the best piece of advice she had ever received, she said, "My mother always used to tell me, 'Do good if you can, to every person you meet, but always make sure you do no harm.' Living by this simple idea has given me great happiness. Each time I meet someone, I try to lift them up in some way by being loving, and then I make sure to do no harm by what I say or do."

She went on to tell me that each one of us either gives or takes life from others when we meet them. "By what we say and do, we can either make someone's day or ruin it. I have always been very careful, especially with what I say. The tongue is like a razor; you can do good or cut someone with your words."

It was not long into these interviews when I began to see that the third secret was not simply to get love, or even to give it to those close to you, but to embody love as a way of being throughout your life. By truly becoming love, we ourselves are transformed. The more we focus on acting with love, the more we find happiness.

A young woman in her late twenties told me a deeply moving story about her mother that is a great witness to the power of the third secret. After her parents came to visit, she took them to the airport, and they boarded their four-hour flight for home. Later that day, her father called. "He told me that on the flight home, my mother had a heart attack as the plane was starting to descend. By the time they landed, she was gone. Two days later, I had to get on a plane to fly home for my mother's funeral."

She recounted for me the long, sad flight home. As she gazed out at the land passing below her, she could not help but wonder what those final moments were like for her mother.

Was she pleased with her life? Had she died with a deep sense of satisfaction or with regret? Was she afraid or at peace? Did she know how much she was loved? Many times, her eyes filled with tears as she tried to catch her breath.

On landing, she headed directly to the funeral home for the visiting hours and discovered a room full of love—of those who had shared her mother's life. Her mother had been a Muslim, but there were people of many faiths and colors. Since the daughter had moved away some time ago, she did not know everyone and kept asking her father who each person was.

There was one woman sitting alone in the corner. When she asked her father who she was, he said he did not know. After asking some of her mother's closest friends, she soon realized that no one seemed to know the middle-aged stranger. She walked up and sat beside the woman and said, "I am her youngest daughter. I am wondering how you knew my mother."

"I am sorry to say that I did not know your mother," the stranger replied.

Perplexed, she asked, "But then why are you here?"

"Many years ago now, I was going through a very difficult time in my life. I was so discouraged that I was thinking very seriously about taking my life. That day, I happened to be riding a bus into the city and sat down next to a woman who was reading a book. Halfway through the bus ride, she put her book down and turned to me. She said, 'You look like a woman who needs to talk.' I don't know why, but she was so kind and so open that I told her what was going on in my life and what I was thinking of doing. When I got home, our time together led me to make a different decision. And that decision has affected not only my life, but the lives of many others."

"But what does this have to do with my mother?" the daughter asked.

"Well, I was so into myself that day that I did not even introduce myself to the woman, did not even know her name. But two days ago, I saw her picture in the paper, and I came here tonight. I did not know your mother. I did not even know her name. But my twenty minutes with her saved my life."

The young woman cried and then smiled. She told me that she realized that her mother had lived her entire life that way. Whether it was with her children, her husband, her many friends, or a stranger she would never meet again, love and kindness had been her way in the world. It had made her a very happy woman, and now her daughter saw it had also made a difference in ways she could not have imagined.

Tom, the Métis native and healer who fell through the ice and found his destiny, told me this: "What I am doing here today, the choice to love, impacts the whole universe. In our tradition, we believe that each act is dispersed for seven generations. Everything we do affects everything else. So when we choose to love, whether our children or a stranger, we change the future."

The third secret is to *become love.*

"*Most people spend life trying to get love. Focus instead on being a loving person. Love always finds loving people.*"

—John Izzo

CHAPTER FOUR

THE FOURTH SECRET:
LIVE THE MOMENT

"Sometimes your joy is the source of your smile,
but sometimes your smile can be the source of
your joy."

—Thich Nhât Hanh

If you listen to two hundred people talk about their lives, you begin to sense the deep common threads of the human journey. Often, people from very different backgrounds use almost identical words to describe their unique human experience.

One of the phrases I heard most often was "it all goes by so fast." Elsa, in her seventies, expressed what many people told me in a variety of ways: "When you are young, sixty years seems like an eternity. But after you have lived it, you realize it is but a moment." We believe we have forever, but we soon realize this is not so.

If life goes by quickly, then one of the secrets to happiness is to get more out of the time we have, to find a way that each moment and each day become great gifts. I came to see that the fourth secret is to *live the moment.*

At its simplest, *live the moment* means to be fully in every moment of our lives, not to judge our lives but to live fully. It means that we must not focus on the past or the future but experience each moment with gratitude and purpose. We have the power in each moment to choose contentment and happiness.

CHOOSING TO BE IN EVERY MOMENT

MAX, IN HIS sixties, told me about a man he encounters each day on his walks with his dog. "He is well into his eighties and still actively involved in a variety of things. When I meet him and ask how he is, he always responds in the same way—with a resoundingly enthusiastic *'I'm here!'* What he really means is 'I am grateful to be alive, and I recognize what a tremendous gift it is.'" Happy people are fully here, wherever they are, whatever they are doing.

Max had been a theater critic for decades and sat through hundreds of performances. He told me about the many performances where it was hard to be fully present. "Sometimes, I would be reviewing a play, and it was so bad that I would think, 'This is an incredible waste of my life.' Then I would realize that I was not going to get those two hours back, so I found something interesting to enjoy in the play. *If we want to live fully, we must banish the word 'boring' from our vocabulary; in each moment, we must simply be fully there and take all that moment has to offer.*"

EVERY
DAY IS
A GIFT

SENECA, THE ROMAN philosopher, said that we should "count each day as a separate life." Each day is not a step on the way to a destination—it is the destination. We begin to *live the moment* when we recognize the great gift of being alive one more day and choose not to squander that single day, not to ruin it by living in the past or the future.

First, we need to make sure that we are *living our life* rather than simply *planning our life*. If we are not careful, we find ourselves forever *getting through things* on our way to what we think will bring us happiness. We may find ourselves continually telling ourselves that we will be *happy if* or that we will be *happy when*. It is not that we should not plan or yearn for things we have not yet achieved or experienced, but rather that happiness is always found when we are able to live in the present moment.

My dog has been one of my best teachers. Each day I am not traveling, my dog, Molly, and I take a walk up the side of the mountain where we live. For forty minutes, we walk straight up and then walk back down. After taking these walks for several years, I came to an interesting realization. My dog was enjoying our walks far more than I was.

For me, the goal was simply to get to the top of the mountain and come back down. The walk was not to be savored but to be gotten through. I was walking to get exercise and hopefully to live a longer life, rather than seeing the walks as important in themselves. Molly, however, enjoyed our walks immensely. If we encountered another dog, she would stop and greet it. If she saw something interesting, she would stop and explore it fully. She spent most of our walks "smelling the roses" while I spent most of our walks imploring her to "come on, let's get going" on my dutiful march to my goal. She was living the moment; I was getting through it.

After coming to this realization, I committed to taking our walks the way she took them. If we meet a neighbor on our walk, I will often stop and have a good conversation; if I catch a mountain vista or see a beautiful flower, I will stop to enjoy it fully; and if I am lucky enough to run into a friend, I take time to catch up instead of getting to my destination. *It has become a metaphor of how I live my life.*

JOHN, A NINETY-THREE-YEAR-OLD painter, talked to me about something he noticed after he turned ninety. "I like to tell people that I am almost ninety-four, much as children might say they are almost eight, because ever since I turned ninety, I have this great appreciation for each day."

He talked about mortality and the limited number of years he had left and how this awareness had begun to shape his daily experience. "When you get to be my age, you are always wondering how long you will live. Now, when I see a beautiful sunset or a performance at the ballet, I cry, not only because it is beautiful, but because I don't know how many more I will get to see. It is important to appreciate each one and each moment as if it might be your last."

The aging painter's words soon became an important image shaping the moments of my life. Each time I found myself in a moment of joy, I began to remind myself that one never knows how many more moments like this will come. *Rather than rushing through such moments, I began to practice breathing them in.*

THE SECOND THING I learned about living in the moment is that the present moment is the only one in which we have any power. If we are to practice the fourth secret, we must choose to live in the present.

Living in the present means recognizing that we have no power over the past or the future. None at all. The past has already occurred and is behind us. Whatever happened, we have no power to change it. Any regrets we had, and any joys, are forever frozen in time. Focusing on the past, especially on regret, only has the power to rob the present moment of its happiness.

But surely we have power over the future? After all, the future has not happened yet. Interestingly, in the present moment, we can do nothing about the future either. Think of how much time we spend worrying about the future. Will I get sick? Will something bad happen to the people I love? Will my children turn out well? Will my company downsize? Worry about the future has only one real power, and that is the power to steal joy.

Of course, how we act in the present moment may influence the future, but all we can do in the present is to be here fully and to know that when tomorrow comes, we will embrace it with the same full energy we give to the moment.

Living in the moment is easy to say but hard to do. Meditation is great practice for training our minds to be present. Practice this. The next time you find yourself lost in regret about the past or worrying about the future, simply tell your mind, "You cannot do anything about the past or the future. Come into the present." If ten minutes later you find yourself doing it again, tell your mind the same thing. Over time, you will find more and more that your mind is fully present in the moment you are in. In that moment, you have power. In that moment, you can take action.

We have the power to train our minds. Most people live their lives with the opposite belief, that somehow our minds are slaves to external circumstances. Happy people know that we are more in control of our minds than most people realize.

Living the moment means we know that at each moment we have the capacity to choose contentment and gratitude. Don, the psychologist who had asked his future wife to dance, talked to me about his changing view on the power he had over his own happiness. "Early in life, I believed that the external world determined how I felt. I would watch a beautiful sunset and experience great delight. Then, when the sun went down, I wondered. Where did that good feeling go? Was it the sun that produced my happiness? I began to realize that the capacity to create that good feeling was within me, not 'out there.'"

He shared a simple formula for living life: *"I have lived by two principles. One is that if something is worth doing, it is worth doing wholeheartedly—don't do something just to get it out of the way. The second thing is that you have the power to shape your thoughts. It is all in your head."*

CRAINING OUR MINDS FOR HAPPINESS

WHEN DON TOLD me that your happiness is ultimately all in your head, a lightbulb began to flicker. The idea that I could, at any given moment, simply choose contentment and gratitude was radical and potentially life-changing. Don was not telling me that this was easy or that it would not require years of practice, only that it was achievable. What the wise ones were telling me was to practice a sweet surrender to life. It was not the surrender of resignation, a mere begrudging acceptance of circumstances; what they were saying was that the power to find happiness was within me, not without. If practiced, I could choose contentment at any time. Slowly, I began a few simple practices: waking up each morning and expressing gratitude; focusing on the good that happened each day before sleep; stopping the incessant worry about the future (and practicing a gentle nudge back to the present moment); and simply practicing breathing in the moments of my life as if they were precious, as if they were numbered. It takes time and practice to learn this secret.

Bill, now in his sixties, said that when he and his siblings were young, his mother would come into their room and wake them up by drawing open the curtains and saying, "Rise and shine. Life is what you make it." Bill admitted, "At the time I hated it, but I think it helped me, because it was a constant reminder that life was not what happened to you; it was how you reacted to it."

Living the moment means choosing to be in a place of gratitude. These wise elders told us again and again that gratitude was the source of fulfillment. Many of them talked about becoming more and more grateful as they aged and less focused on what they did not have. Gratitude emerged not as a mere attitude but a core "life philosophy."

Several years ago, I gave a talk to a large audience. A young man in his early thirties was sitting in the first row. All through my talk, he listened intently. He took a great many notes, laughed loudly when something was humorous, and cried openly when I told a touching story. After my talk, he asked if I would sign one of my books. While I was signing, he thanked me for my "great talk," but I said, "No, I want to thank you."

I continued: "You had such great energy, and all through my talk, I found myself getting energized just by looking at you. And there you were, sitting right in the first row."

"I learned that from my grandmother," he said. "When she died last year, there were no tears of grief at her funeral. There was sadness and a great deal of laughter, but when my grandmother died, we knew she had taken everything life had to give—every pleasure, every moment fully lived, every day. So I learned from watching my grandmother that if you sit in the front row everywhere you are, every day and in every moment, you will die a happy person."

When we wake up, we should say "thank you" for one more day and ask that we not waste it. When people meet us, we should greet them with an enthusiastic "I'm here," sending a prayer to our subconscious of presence and gratitude. Whenever we find our minds drifting to the regret of yesterday or worry about tomorrow, we gently bring our minds into the present moment. All during the day, we should appreciate each small pleasure, because it might be our last. And at the end of the day, we'll recount all the good things that happened, however small, and ask for one more day.

The fourth secret is to *live the moment.*

"We must train our minds for happiness, since it is not out there where joy is found, but in our capacity to be in the moment, fully aware and grateful."

—John Izzo

CHAPTER FIVE

THE FIFTH SECRET:
Give More than You Take

"Life is no brief candle to me. It is a sort of splendid torch which I have got hold of for the moment, and I want to make it burn as brightly as I can before handing it on to future generations."

—George Bernard Shaw

Many years ago, when I was a young clergyman, I conducted a funeral for a man I had not known. I will never forget the day of his funeral, as I stood before a closed coffin and gave a eulogy without an audience. Although the man had lived in that county most of his life and his two adult sons lived only a few hours away, not one person came to celebrate his life. Only the funeral director and I were in attendance. At the time, I was only twenty-five, but the experience had a profound effect on me. How, I wondered, could a person live so long and touch so few people?

As I learned more about the man's life, I realized that he lived a life focused almost entirely on his own needs. For most of his later years, he had been extremely bitter, and whatever light he brought into the world had died with him.

His funeral was a symbol of his life; as he lived, so he died.

My own grandfather's funeral was an entirely different experience. When the day came for his funeral, the family was surprised at how many people were in attendance. He had been a quiet man, and yet scores of strangers came up to my mother to tell her what a difference my grandfather had made in their lives. The funeral director apologized for holding the visiting hours in a room too small for the life my grandfather had obviously lived. At the funeral home, one man told my mother that one day, he was standing outside a dress shop, looking at an Easter dress for his daughter, a dress he could not afford. My grandfather passed by the shop and, after a brief conversation, insisted on buying it, even though he had little money. He said, "Pay me back when you can." Scores of people had gathered, not because of what my grandfather had taken from the world, but because of what he had given.

We routinely talked to the wise interviewees about their lives. One question we asked was "What has given your life the greatest sense of purpose and meaning?" What I discovered in listening to their answers is the fifth and final secret we must discover before we die—*give more than you take.*

TEN-MINUTE FUNERALS AND TEN-HOUR FUNERALS

PEOPLE KEPT TELLING me that what really mattered in life was what you left behind, that something was different because you were here. The ways people felt their lives had mattered varied greatly, but the theme kept recurring. For some people, it was having lived long enough to see their children grow into healthy adults who were living loving and useful lives. Others looked back on the good work they had done and how this work would affect the future. For still others, it was simply the knowledge that by giving more than they took in their daily lives, they had somehow stumbled onto happiness. As we listened to these people, we realized that it is those who give the most who find the greatest joy.

Ken, the barber, listened to the stories of those whose hair he had cut and found a way to be of service.

"What I discovered is that the greatest happiness you find in life is always from what you give, not what you get. These people who come into my barber shop live hard lives working the soil. For a half hour, I get to serve them, help them relax, and do something for them. Being a barber is like being a priest; people come in and tell you about their lives. You listen, and in some way, you try to help. The greatest pleasure in life is seeing that you made something better."

Ken told me that he attended a great many funerals. "What I noticed is that there are ten-minute funerals and ten-hour funerals. Some people live a life that touches so many people in a positive way that people just want to hang around and talk about that person's life. Other people live a more self-focused life, and this does not happen. It seems to me you should live your life as if you want a ten-hour funeral."

The more I listened, the more I realized that happy people are always *givers not takers*. *They may not have been as selfless as Mother Teresa or Gandhi, but they discovered that the more we give, the more we find happiness.*

ASK

WHAT LIFE EXPECTS OF YOU

ONE OF THE reasons *giving more than we take* is one of the secrets to happiness and purpose is because we have a great deal of control over what we give (but almost none over what we get). Each day, we have the power to give without limit. We can choose kindness, to serve, to love, to be generous, and to leave the world better in some way. I came to believe that there is something in us as human beings that longs to make a contribution while we are here.

Antony, eighty-six, had been an actor his entire life and was still performing and directing. From the moment we met, it was clear to me that he had lived the five secrets. He had found work he loved and followed his heart. He made room for love and had given love to others. Although he enjoyed applause and the accolades, he told me that what really mattered was seeing how he had influenced people.

"When I was young, it was all about getting the part. But as you get older, you want to know your work mattered. Recently, I starred as Morrie in the play *Tuesdays with Morrie*, and the reviews were great. But what meant the most to me was a letter I received from a young man who attended the show. He was visiting with his family from Korea and wrote to tell me that it was the first play he had ever seen and my performance had changed his view about life and what really mattered. That letter meant more to me than all the applause."

The actor reminded me that we often don't realize for many years how our life has made a difference. He told me a wonderful story about an experience he had with a former student.

"Earlier in my life, I taught acting while in England, and although I always enjoyed acting more than teaching, I believe I made a real difference for students. Perhaps it is because I did not try to get them to act *my* way but tried to help them discover their own style."

Almost forty years after moving to Canada, he returned to England with his wife and was contacted by a former student. The student asked if he might take them to dinner while they were in London. When Antony and his wife arrived, they realized it was a very, very expensive gourmet restaurant.

They had a great dinner and good conversation, catching up. When the bill arrived, Antony asked to contribute because he knew it was a large tab. But Kenny took the bill.

"No, I insist on paying," Kenny said. "Don't you realize that everything I have in my life I owe to you! Your teaching changed my life. You lit a fire in me for acting and taught me what it means to be a professional. Your teaching is what made me a success."

Although Antony had fond memories of his former pupil, he had no idea what a difference he had made in his student's life. "Often, we don't find out for many years and sometimes never. It had such an effect on me to realize that I had made such an impact on his life."

This is true for each one of us. We often see only the tip of the iceberg in terms of the difference we make during our lifetime. *We make a difference, even when we do not know it.*

THE GREAT TASK OF LIFE: LOSE YOURSELF

THERE ARE TWO great tasks of a human life—*to find ourselves* and *to lose ourselves*. We find ourselves by discovering our destiny and being true to ourselves. Yet it is not enough to find ourselves; we also must lose ourselves.

The loss of self is about seeing that we are connected to something much larger, something that had a life before us and that will have a life after us. We are significant because we are part of a larger entity. For some, this is God; for some, it is the human journey; and for others, all of nature. What I found is that those who both found themselves and lost themselves found happiness. There is no better way to lose ourselves than to dedicate our life to giving, to leaving the world better than we found it. This connects us to the future and links us to the past.

As I listened to many voices of people near the end of their lives, I realized that we are all a part of a much larger chain of life. We ultimately find happiness by joining that larger story, focusing less on ourselves and our small concerns and joining something wider and grander. Many of the spiritual traditions focus on this paradox: that it is only by surrendering the ego, the focus on self, that we find true happiness.

As I listened to the perspectives of people over sixty, I became increasingly aware that we live in a borrowed world. Each generation borrows the world from the one that came before it and holds it in trust for those yet to arrive. Each generation is a steward of this great gift while it is ours. Happiness comes both from giving and a deep sense of responsibility to the future.

Chief Ralph, in his sixties, was the elected leader of an aboriginal group on Vancouver Island in western Canada. He told me a beautiful story about an experience he had as a teenager.

"We lived on the Pacific Ocean, and each year, there was a large salmon run. We all looked forward to going out on the boat and catching fish, which we needed for food during the winter. One year, my brothers and I went out on the boat with my father early in the morning. The fish were so plentiful that in only a few short hours the boat was loaded with salmon, and we had to come back. We three brothers were so excited and hurried to get the fish off the boat so we could go out and catch more."

Chief Ralph continued, "When we told our father that we were ready to go out again, he said, 'No, we are finished.' We asked him why. We knew there were many more fish to catch. But my father said, 'We must leave some for others.' We spent the next two days helping other tribe members mend their nets so they too could have enough. That is what I remember."

These teenagers represent so much of what we believe to be true early in our lives. We set out to catch as many fish as we can. We believe that happiness will be found in the number of experiences we have or possessions we gain. Later, often too late, we discover that love, service, and connection to a larger purpose are the true food of the human soul. Ralph's father knew that he lived in a borrowed world. It was important to take enough to eat, but it was also important to take no more than was needed.

The fish did not belong to his family or even to his community. The fish were borrowed from generations past and held in trust for many generations yet to come. *His father, I suspected, knew that the most important lesson he had to give his teenage sons was not a lesson in fishing technique, but that giving to others was the greatest pleasure a human being can have.*

LEARN

TO CRY FOR THE WORLD, NOT FOR YOURSELF

SUSAN, SIXTY-EIGHT, TOLD me that "as I have aged, I find I no longer cry for myself, but I cry for the world. Part of getting older is realizing you will not be here forever but that the story goes on beyond you." The happiest people we interviewed had learned to cry for the world, and those who were most unhappy were still crying for themselves. We can learn this lesson when we are young or in midlife: our greatest happiness will come from what we give away.

"What matters is how we treat each other," Susan told me, "and how we interact with the environment. We must think about our impact on the future."

Perhaps happiness cannot really be pursued. Perhaps it is a by-product of something more profound. Juana, sixty-four, said, "If you are unhappy, get busy doing something for someone else. If you concentrate on yourself, you will be unhappy, but if you focus on helping others, you will find happiness. Happiness comes from serving and loving."

The happiest people I interviewed knew their life had mattered, that they had been of service. The most miserable people had focused on themselves and finding happiness, getting love, and accumulating things, status, and fame.

But does each one of us really have the capability to change the world? Each one of us changes the movement of the world based on how we interact with it. Taken together, these subtle changes shape the future.

I recall vividly the first time I really saw the Milky Way. Having grown up in a large urban area, I rarely saw more than a few stars at night. But in college, I went on to do a work tour on the islands of Bermuda. One night, around midnight, we walked to the top of a hill and lay down on the grass, facing the dark night sky. There above me was the Milky Way, a part of the sky so dense with stars that it looked like the Creator had thrown milk across the sky.

As I was admiring the sky, I remembered something I had learned in an astronomy class: many of the stars we see at night may no longer exist. They are so far away from our earth that it takes millions of years for their light to reach us. I was seeing the light of some stars that were already extinguished.

At nineteen, I remember thinking that some people's lives were like that, shining a light in the world long after they were gone. *I said a prayer that I would live that kind of life.*

The fifth secret is to **give more than we take.** When we give more than we take, we connect ourselves to a story bigger than ourselves. In the act of doing so, happiness finds us.

CHAPTER SIX

A Final Lesson:

It's Never too Late to Live the Secrets

"The best day to plant a tree was twenty years ago.
The second best time is now."

—Chinese Proverb

The most important thing is not *when* we find the secrets but *that we do* find the secrets. No matter what age we are, or what mistakes we have made, when we embrace and live the five secrets, our lives begin to change.

Living our life means that we take our life day to day and moment to moment, always trying to deepen our understanding of what it means to be human. Life will never be perfect, and we will always be in a state of moving toward completeness. It is never too late to embrace the five secrets found in this book and to change the legacy of many years. Even one year lived wisely can erase many years of regret.

John, the ninety-three-year-old painter from Toronto, said, "You cannot live in regret; you did what you did to the best of your ability at the time. Sometimes I talk to people who are in their forties or fifties, and they are already talking as if their lives were almost over. But I want to tell them, 'Look you have only been an adult for twenty or twenty-five years. It is not very much time to figure life out. And if you live to be my age, you may have another entire adult lifetime, or maybe two, before you die. So don't give up on yourself.'"

It is my hope that each person who reads this book will experience the same grace and perspective that these wise people offered me. Stop judging the life you have lived and get on with the life you still may live. Whatever mistakes you have made, and no matter how many regrets may litter your past, plant a new tree today. Begin to live the secrets now or simply live them more deeply. This is what the wise elders wanted me to know.

An award-winning writer and author, corporate culture crusader, and global sustainability advocate, John Izzo, PhD, has devoted his life and career to facilitating deeper conversations about personal values, work culture, life fulfillment, leadership responsibility, and the true definition of success.

Izzo obtained his bachelor's in sociology from Hofstra University and completed dual master's degree programs in theology from McCormick Divinity School and organizational psychology from the University of Chicago. He went on to earn his PhD in organizational communication from Kent State University. Izzo has served on the faculty of three major universities and is the past board chair of the Sierra Club and the Canadian Parks and Wilderness Society.

Dr. Izzo has shared platforms around the world with politicians, environmentalists, corporate icons, foundation heads, and movie magnates, including Ken Blanchard, Bill Clinton, David Suzuki, Oprah Winfrey, Peter Mansbridge, and Jane Fonda, and he is asked to speak to more than one hundred audiences each year. He has authored and published more than six hundred articles and is the author of four national bestselling books: *Second Innocence*, *Values Shift*, *Awakening Corporate Soul*, and *Stepping Up*.

Fast Company, CNN, Wisdom Network, Canada AM, ABC World News, *Working Woman*, *Wall Street Journal*, *McLean's*, and *Inc.* have featured the research and opinions of John Izzo.

In 2007, the Biography Channel and Dr. Izzo filmed a five-part series called "The Five Things You Must Discover Before You Die."

Born and raised on the East Coast of the United States, Dr. Izzo now lives in Vancouver, British Columbia, Canada. For more information on Dr. John Izzo and his colleagues, visit **www.drjohnizzo.com.**